My Bible Friends

To

Brian and Bruce
Randy and Diana

And

all the boys and girls
who like Bible stories

Published jointly by
REVIEW AND HERALD® PUBLISHING ASSOCIATION
Hagerstown, MD 21740

PACIFIC PRESS PUBLISHING ASSOCIATION
Boise, ID 83707

ISBN 0-8280-1014-5
Library of Congress Catalog Card No. 76-55834

PRINTED IN U.S.A.

My Bible Friends

Etta B. Degering/Book One

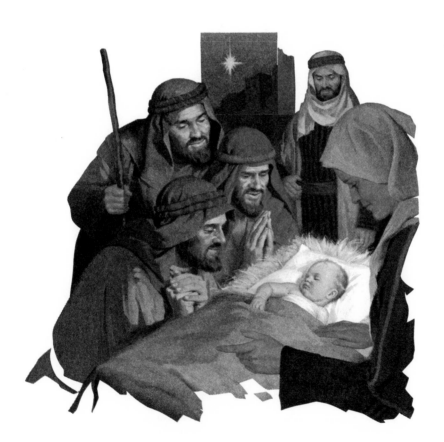

The stories in this book are—

Baby Moses	Joseph's New Coat
Baby Jesus	Joseph and His Brothers

Baby Moses

(Exodus 2)

Moses was a wee baby boy.
His Mother loved him
    and held him close.
His Father loved him
    and patted his fat cheeks.
Sister Miriam loved him
    and sang him happy songs.
Little Brother loved him
    and tickled his tiny toes.
Never was a baby more loved than Baby Moses.

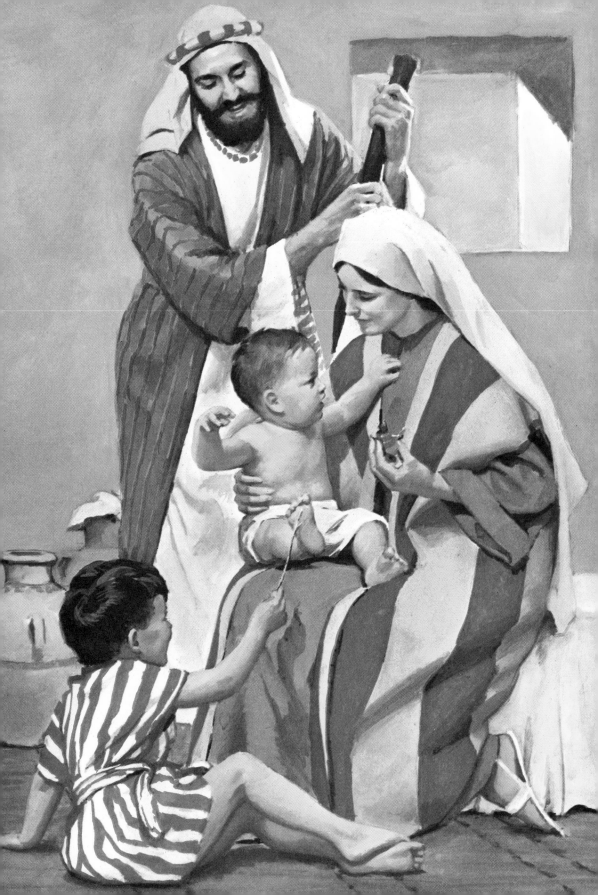

But the king where Moses lived was a wicked man.
He said to his helpers,
    "Throw all the baby boys into the river."
"Oh, no, no!" said Mother,
    and held Baby Moses closer.
"We'll never let anyone throw our baby
    into the river," said Father.
"No, never, never!" said Miriam.
    Little Brother shook his head, *"No!"*

"We'll hide our baby," said Mother.
But Baby Moses didn't like
    to be hidden away all day—
    he cried and cried.
Miriam was afraid the king's men would hear.
"Sh! Sh! Baby Moses," she whispered,
    but he cried the louder.
"Oh, what can we do?" asked Miriam.

"We'll make a basket boat for Baby Moses
     and hide him in the rushes
     at the river's edge," said Mother.
They wove a tight little basket
     and painted it with pitch
     to keep it from leaking.
Mother put a soft pillow in it.
She laid Baby Moses on the soft pillow.

Early the next morning—so early Little Brother
was not yet awake—Mother and Miriam
took the little boat with Baby Moses in it
down to the river.
They floated it on the water.

Tall rushes kept the basket boat from floating away.
Mother left Miriam to watch
   while she went home and prayed God
   to keep her baby safe.
The sun shone warm.
The soft breezes blew.
The water rocked the little boat.
Baby Moses liked to be rocked.
He fell fast asleep.

Miriam hid in the bushes by the river.
She watched the basket boat
   as it rocked to and fro on the water.
But listen! Someone was coming.
Oh! Oh! Oh!
It was the king's daughter and her maids
   coming to bathe in the river.
Would she see the little boat?
Would *she* throw Baby Moses into the river?

The king's daughter came closer and closer.
She stopped at the river's edge
   and pointed to the little boat.
"Go," she said to her maid,
   "go bring the basket to me."
The king's daughter raised the cover.
"Oh, what a lovely baby!" she said.
   "I want him for my very own."

Miriam came running.
She made a little bow to the king's daughter.
   "Shall I get a nurse for the baby?"
"Yes," said the king's daughter, "go find a nurse
   to take care of the baby for me."
Miriam bowed again, and then she ran home
   as fast as she could go.
"Mother, Mother! Come, come!
The king's daughter found Baby Moses.
She wants a nurse for him.
She likes our baby.
She won't let anyone throw him into the river."

Mother and Miriam hurried to the river.
There stood the king's daughter holding Baby Moses.
He was crying—he was afraid of the strange lady.
"Take this baby and nurse him for me;
I will pay you wages," said the king's daughter.
Mother held out her arms for the baby.
Baby Moses smiled and held up his hands.
The king's daughter said to Mother,
   "Keep the baby for me until he is a big boy."

Mother took Baby Moses, and started up the path.
She was happy to be taking her baby home.
Now she wouldn't have to hide him any more.
Miriam was so happy she skipped and sang.
Baby Moses laughed and cooed. He was happy too.
Father and Little Brother were waiting for them.
Little Brother jumped up and down and waved.

When all were safely in their home again,
    they all kneeled in prayer
    around Baby Moses' cradle—
    Father, Mother, Miriam, and Little Brother.
"Thank You, God," prayed Father,
    "thank You for keeping our baby safe."

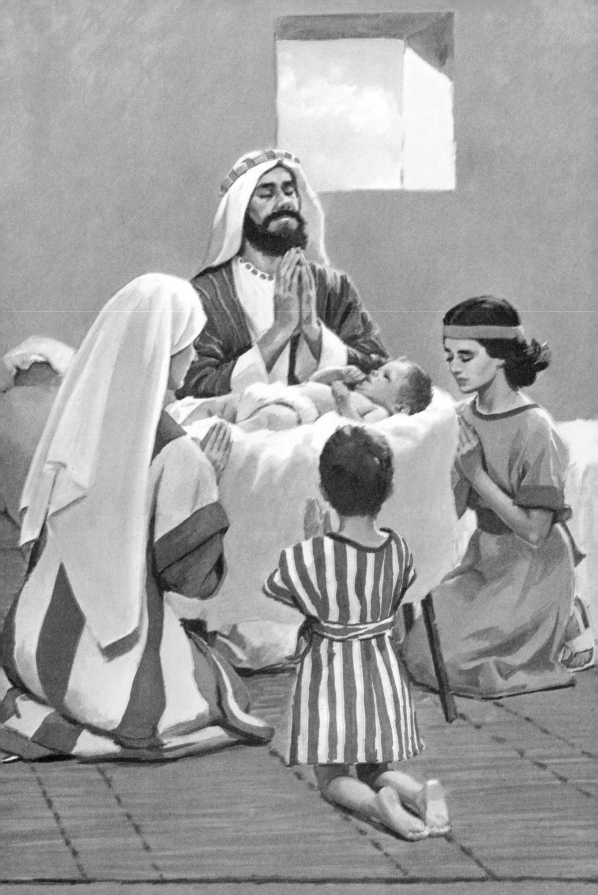

Baby Jesus

(Matthew 2, Luke 2)

Clip ——— clop ——— clip ——— clop,
    went Small Donkey's hoofs
    as he s-l-o-w-l-y climbed the last hill.
Mary rode on Small Donkey's back.
Joseph walked by Small Donkey's side.
Mary and Joseph were very, very tired.
Small Donkey was tired, too.
They had come a long, long way.
From the top of the hill, O happy sight,
    they saw the lights of Bethlehem!

Joseph walked faster now.
Clip-clop, clip-clop, clip-clop, hurried Small Donkey,
    down the hill, through the gate,
    into the little town,
    where they would rest and sleep.
At the inn, Joseph asked for a room.
"We have no room," said the innkeeper.
"Is there no place where we can sleep?" asked Joseph.
"Only in the stable. . . . I am sorry."

Joseph led Small Donkey toward the stable.
He opened the creaky old door.
He held up the lantern the innkeeper gave him,
    and looked around inside.
He saw Spotted Cow, and Woolly Lamb,
    and stalls that were empty.
In one empty stall he tied Small Donkey.
In another he made a bed of straw
    for Mary and himself.
Soon they were fast asleep.

During the night the most wonderful thing happened—
    Baby Jesus was born!
Joseph filled a manger with clean new hay.
Mary wrapped the baby in soft white cloth,
    and laid Him in the manger.
The animals seemed pleased about Baby Jesus.
Spotted Cow mooed softly,
    Woolly Lamb tinkled his bell,
    and Small Donkey looked and looked.

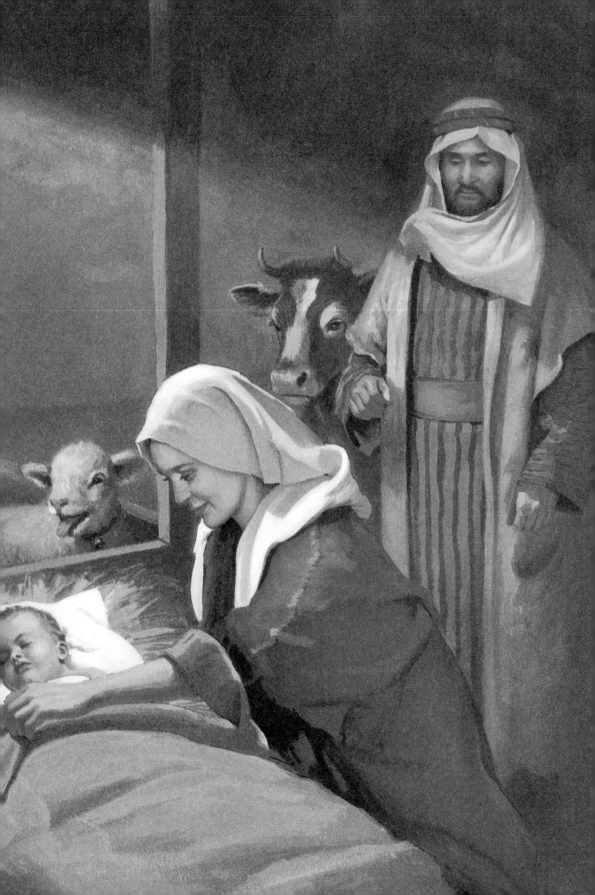

That night, in a field near the little town,
    shepherds were guarding their sheep.
Suddenly a bright light, as bright as the sun,
    shone all around them.
The shepherds were afraid
    and covered their faces.
The sheep were afraid
    and huddled together.

"Don't be afraid," said a kind, gentle voice.
The shepherds uncovered their faces.
They saw an angel, all glowing with light.
Said the angel, "I bring you good tidings of great joy!
    Jesus, your Saviour, is born.
    You will find Him lying in a manger."
Then the sky was filled with shining angels
    singing the glory song—
"*Glory to God in the highest, and on earth peace,
    good will toward men.*"

As the angels went farther and farther away,
    they looked like a twinkling bright star
    in the dark night sky above Bethlehem.
"Come," said the shepherds, "let us go see."
They ran all the way to the stable, and there
    they found Joseph and Mary and
    Baby Jesus in His manger bed.

In a faraway country, Wise Men saw the angel star.
They said, "It is the star of the Baby King.
   Let us go worship Him, and take Him presents."
The Wise Men made ready their gifts.
   One Wise Man filled a bag with gold.
   Another filled a jar with frankincense,
     the perfume of flowers.
   And another filled a special box with myrrh,
     the perfume of spices.

The Wise Men gathered up their gifts,
    mounted their camels,
    and rode toward the star.
They crossed rivers and hills and **sandy deserts**—
    sometimes it was hot,
    sometimes it was cold,
    but always they rode on, following the star.

Then one evening the star stopped above a house
    in the little town of Bethlehem.
The Wise Men made their camels kneel
    in front of the house.
They climbed off the camels' humped backs,
    and taking their gifts,
      they knocked on the door.

Joseph opened the door—and there inside
    was Mary holding Baby Jesus.
The Wise Men bowed with their faces to the floor
    and worshiped the baby they called king.
They gave Him their gifts—
    the bag of gold,
    the jar of frankincense,
    the special box of myrrh.
Then the Wise Men said good-by, mounted their camels,
    and began their long journey home.

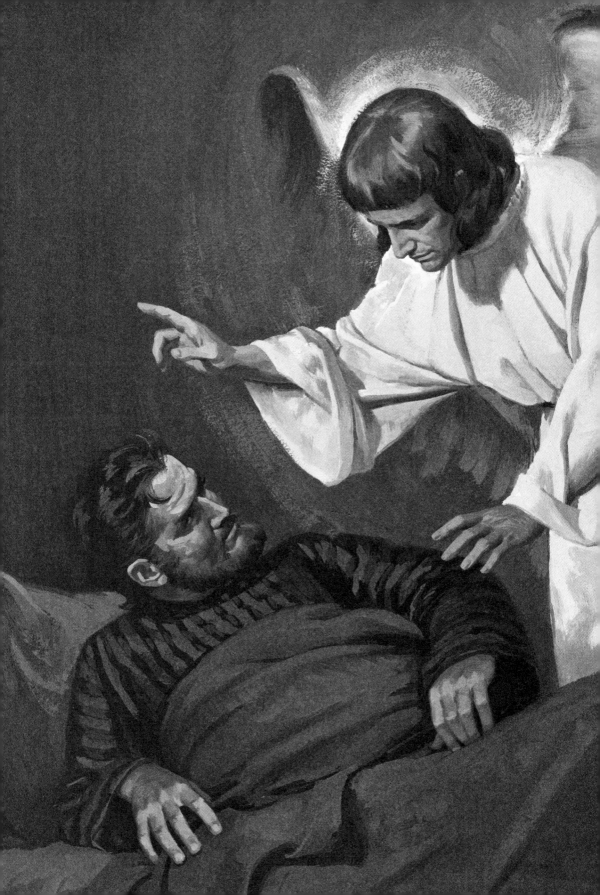

One dark night when Joseph was asleep,
    and Mary was asleep,
    and Baby Jesus was asleep,
    an angel whispered to Joseph.
"Get up quickly," he said. "Take Mary and the Baby
    and flee into Egypt. The wicked king
    is trying to find the Baby to do Him harm.
Stay in Egypt until I tell you it is safe to return."
The king was angry because the people were saying
    that some day Baby Jesus would be king.

Joseph got up quickly.

He told Mary what the angel had said.

He went to the stable for Small Donkey.

Mary wrapped Baby Jesus snug and warm.

Joseph helped Mary on Small Donkey's back.

He handed her Baby Jesus.

Clip-clop, clip-clop, went Small Donkey's hoofs

as they went out through Bethlehem's gate,

and turned down the road toward Egypt.

The wicked king couldn't find Baby Jesus now.

Joseph and Mary, Baby Jesus, and Small Donkey
    lived in Egypt a long time.
Baby Jesus learned to walk and to talk.
Then one night the angel again whispered to Joseph,
    "The wicked king is dead. It is safe to go home."
Once more Mary rode on Small Donkey's back,
    but the Boy Jesus didn't ride all the way now.
Sometimes He walked and helped to lead Small Donkey.
They didn't go to Bethlehem where Jesus was born.
They went to Nazareth, Joseph and Mary's old home.

Joseph and Mary were glad to be back in their old home.
Small Donkey was glad to be back in his own stable.
When Mary tucked the Boy Jesus into His own bed,
 she told Him good-night stories.
She told about—
 Baby Moses and his basket boat,
 about when the angels sang the glory song,
 about the Wise Men following the star,
 and worshiping the Baby as their king.

Joseph's New Coat
(Genesis 37)

Joseph lived in a tent,
    a large striped tent
    out in the country.
Jacob, his father, owned many, many sheep.
Joseph's ten big brothers herded the sheep
    on the hills round about.
Joseph and little brother Benjamin
    took care of the lambs
    that had no mothers.

Joseph and Benjamin fed the lambs
    from little clay bowls.
They put their fingers down into the warm milk
    and let the lambs suck their fingers.
The lambs' tails wiggle-waggled up,
    and wiggle-waggled down,
    as they drank their milk.
It was the lambs' way of saying,
    "The milk is good,
    so warm and good."

It was springtime.
The days were sunny and warm,
    too warm for a coat.
Joseph folded his coat neatly
    and put it away.
He wouldn't need it
    until the chilly winds blew again.
The sheep were too warm in their woolly coats.
    "Baa-a-a-a! Baa-a-a-a!" they called.
    "We want our coats off too."

"It's time to shear the sheep," said Jacob.
Joseph and Benjamin brought the clipping shears.
The big brothers laid the sheep down
      on the cool green grass.
Clip, clip, went the clipping shears.
The sheep were as quiet as could be
      while they were getting their wool cut.
The brothers tied the wool into bundles
      and put it away.

The sheep looked different
    with their woolly coats off.
The lambs didn't know their mothers.
They ran here—they ran there. They cried,
    "Baa-a-a-a! Baa-a-a-a!
    Where's my mother?"
But soon the mother sheep found
    their lost little lambs,
    just as Joseph and Benjamin knew they would.

During the bright summer days the lambs grew
     almost as big as their mothers.
Joseph grew taller and bigger.
Benjamin grew bigger too.
By the time the chilly winds began to blow,
     the sheep had grown new wool coats.
Joseph went to get his coat—but—Oh, Oh, Oh!
     his coat, his warm winter coat,
     was now far too small.

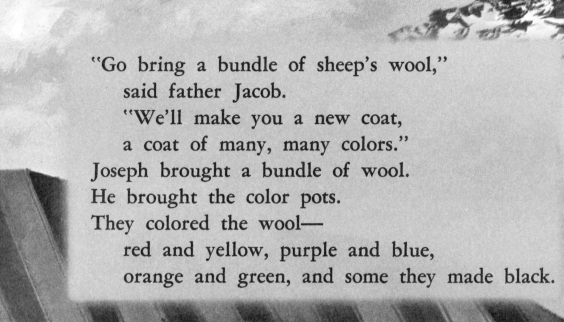

"Go bring a bundle of sheep's wool,"
    said father Jacob.
    "We'll make you a new coat,
    a coat of many, many colors."
Joseph brought a bundle of wool.
He brought the color pots.
They colored the wool—
    red and yellow, purple and blue,
    orange and green, and some they made black.

They twirled the wool on smooth spinning sticks
    and made it into fine wool thread.
Jacob twirled, Joseph twirled.
Twirl—twirl—whirl—whirl,
    went the spinning sticks.
Longer, longer, grew the thread.
Benjamin wound the wool thread onto spools.

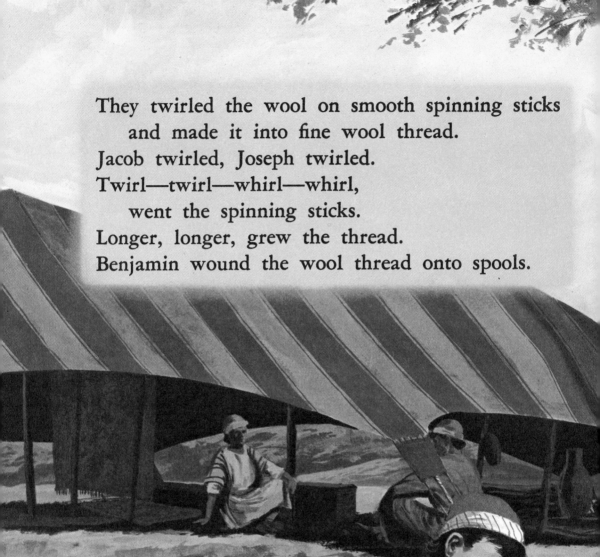

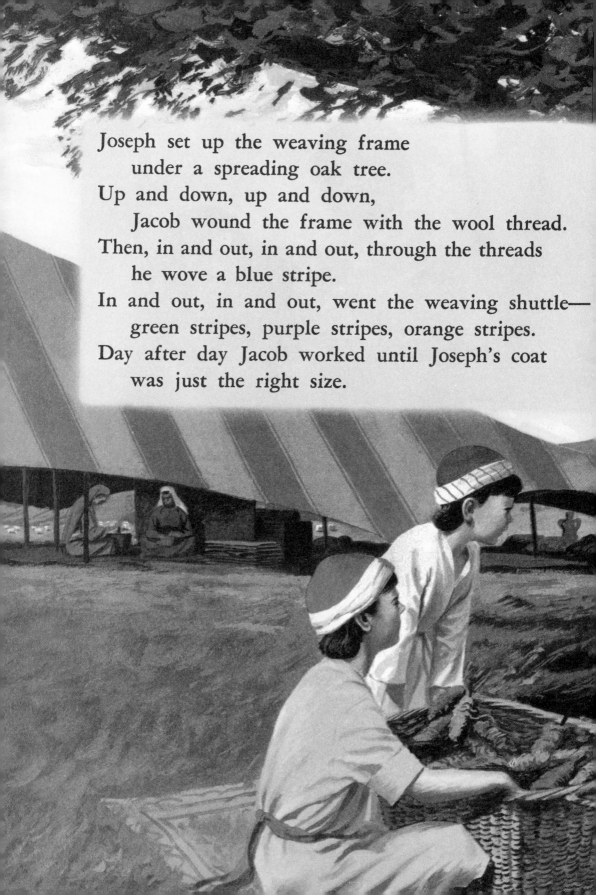

Joseph set up the weaving frame
  under a spreading oak tree.
Up and down, up and down,
  Jacob wound the frame with the wool thread.
Then, in and out, in and out, through the threads
  he wove a blue stripe.
In and out, in and out, went the weaving shuttle—
  green stripes, purple stripes, orange stripes.
Day after day Jacob worked until Joseph's coat
  was just the right size.

Joseph tried on his new coat of many colors.
It was long like a man's. It had sleeves.
"It fits you, my son, it fits you!" said Jacob,
    well pleased with their work.
"It's a p-r-e-t-t-y coat!" said Benjamin.
"It's a fine warm coat," said Joseph.
    "Thank you my father, and brother."

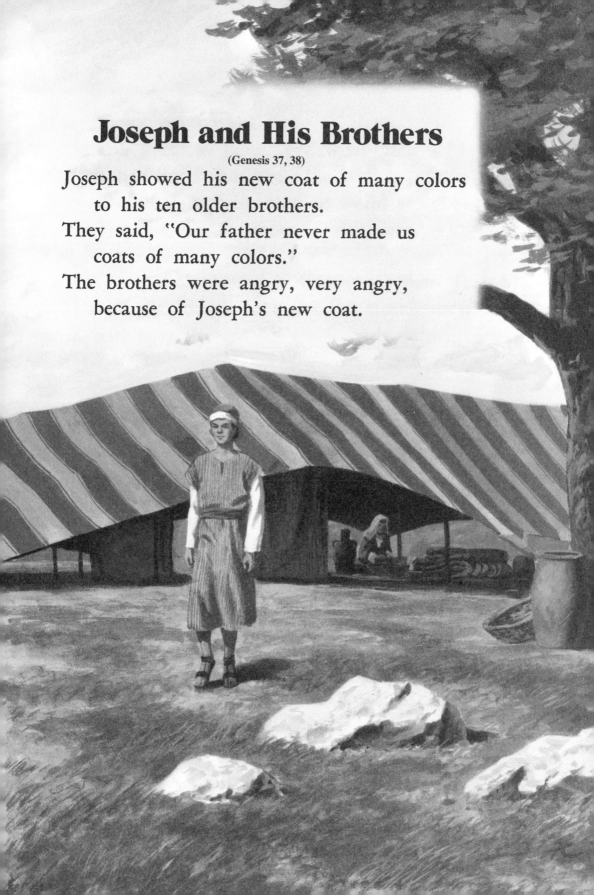

Joseph and His Brothers

(Genesis 37, 38)

Joseph showed his new coat of many colors
to his ten older brothers.

They said, "Our father never made us
coats of many colors."

The brothers were angry, very angry,
because of Joseph's new coat.

One night while Joseph lay sleeping
  he dreamed a dream—a strange dream.
He dreamed he and his brothers were in the field
  tying sheaves of wheat.
Suddenly his sheaf stood up straight and tall.
His brothers' sheaves gathered around
  and bowed to his sheaf.

Joseph told his brothers the strange dream.
They said, "Do you think we are going
  to bow down to you?"
The brothers were angry, very angry,
  because of Joseph's strange dream.

Joseph's brothers went to a faraway place
    to find green grass for the sheep.
When they had been gone a long time,
    father Jacob said to Joseph,
    "Go see if your brothers are well,
    and if it be well with the sheep."
Joseph put on his coat of many colors.
He said good-by to his father.
He said good-by to his little brother Benjamin.
Then he began the long, long walk.
Joseph walked, and walked, and walked.
At last, from the top of a hill,
    he saw his brothers and the sheep
    camped by the road that leads to Egypt.

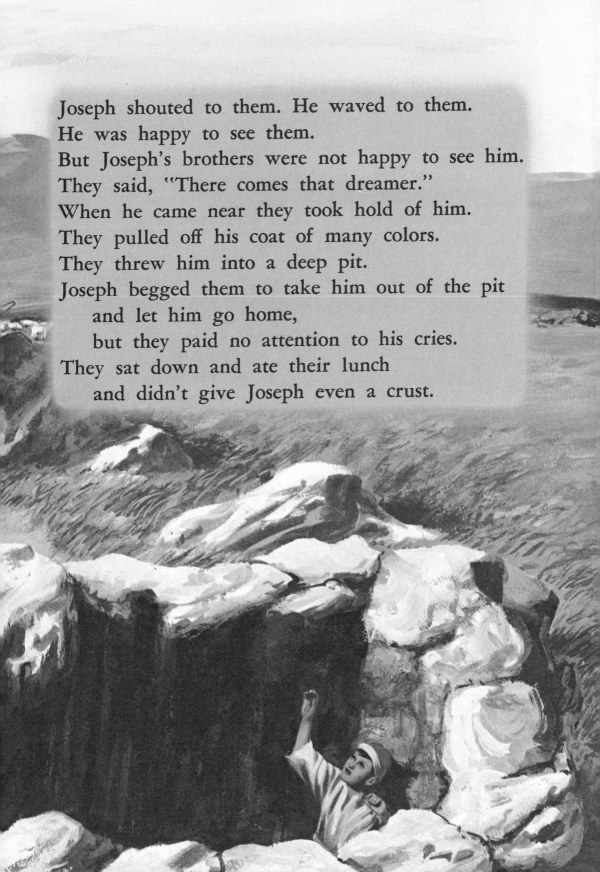

Joseph shouted to them. He waved to them.
He was happy to see them.
But Joseph's brothers were not happy to see him.
They said, "There comes that dreamer."
When he came near they took hold of him.
They pulled off his coat of many colors.
They threw him into a deep pit.
Joseph begged them to take him out of the pit
    and let him go home,
    but they paid no attention to his cries.
They sat down and ate their lunch
    and didn't give Joseph even a crust.

Down the dusty road that leads to Egypt
    came traders with their camels.
Said the brothers,
    "Let's sell Joseph to the traders."
So they took Joseph up out of the pit
    and sold him for twenty pieces of silver.

The traders took Joseph and went on their way.
From the road, Joseph could see the hills
    where his father's tent was pitched.
He knew Benjamin was there with his father.
If only he could be there too.
Joseph cried, and cried, and cried.
Then Joseph stopped crying.
He said, "I will be brave.
    God will take care of me."

Down in Egypt the traders sold Joseph
    to a man named Potiphar.
Joseph had to work hard.
His legs got tired, his back got tired,
    but he did his work well.
When he swept the floor he was careful
    to sweep in the corners.
When he pulled weeds in the garden
    he pulled every one.
Potiphar said, "You are a good worker, Joseph."

Joseph learned to talk like the people of Egypt.
He wore clothes like the people of Egypt.
He cut his hair like the people of Egypt.
But there was one thing he would never,
 never do like the people of Egypt.
The people of Egypt prayed to an idol,
 or to a cat, and sometimes even to a frog.
But Joseph prayed always to the God of heaven,
 as Jacob his father had taught him.

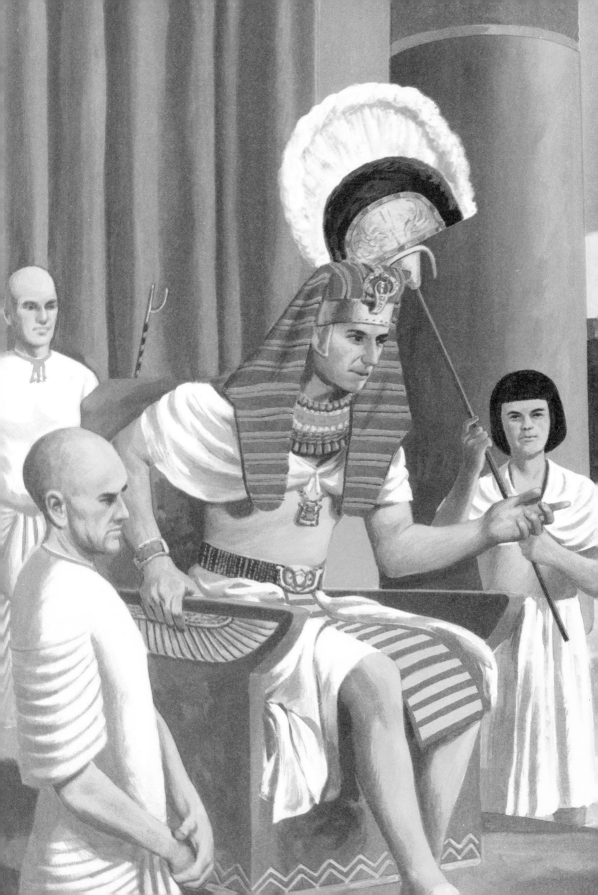

Many many years went by.

Joseph grew to be a very wise man.

Now it happened that the king of Egypt
wanted a very wise man to build storehouses
and to fill the storehouses with corn.

The king said,

"Where could I find a man wiser than Joseph?
I will get Joseph to build the storehouses.
I will have Joseph fill them with corn."

So the king made Joseph ruler of Egypt
    next to himself.
He said to the people of Egypt,
    "Whatever Joseph says, you must do."
Joseph rode in a shiny chariot.
He drove a team of prancing horses.
Joseph built the storehouses for the king.
He filled the storehouses with corn.

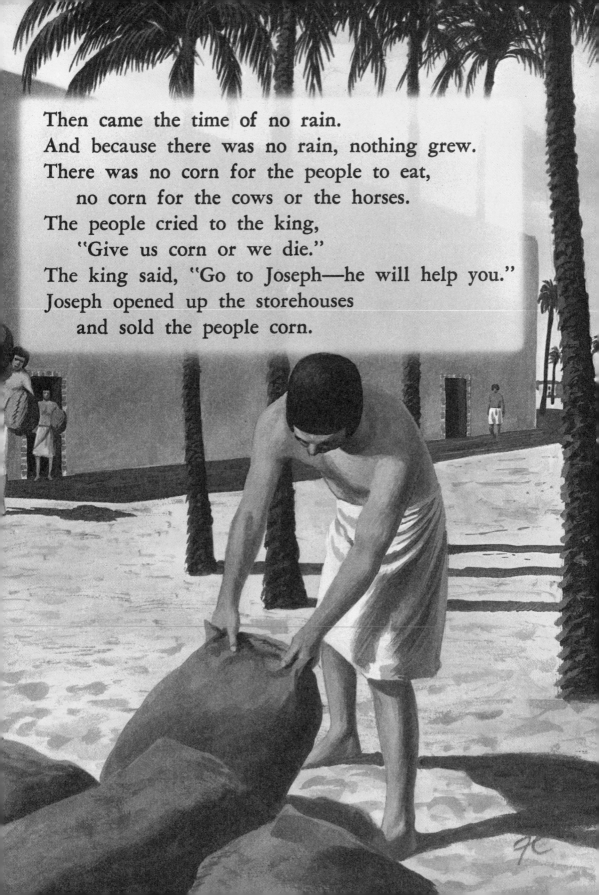

Then came the time of no rain.
And because there was no rain, nothing grew.
There was no corn for the people to eat,
    no corn for the cows or the horses.
The people cried to the king,
    "Give us corn or we die."
The king said, "Go to Joseph—he will help you."
Joseph opened up the storehouses
    and sold the people corn.

One day Joseph saw ten little donkeys
    with empty sacks on their backs
    coming toward the storehouse
    where he was selling corn.
Beside the ten little donkeys
    walked his ten older brothers.
The brothers didn't know Joseph,
    but Joseph knew them.
They bowed to Joseph with their faces to the ground.
Joseph remembered his dream about the sheaves.

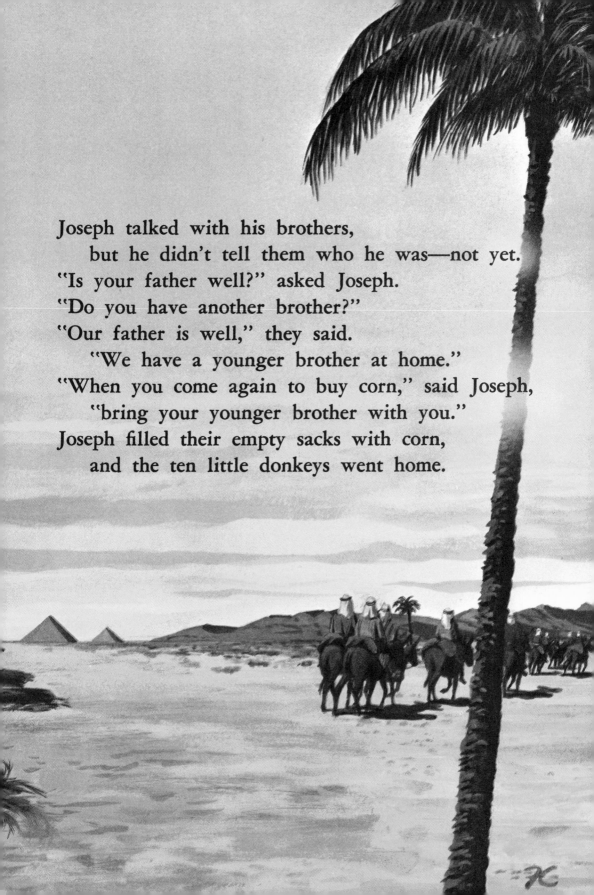

Joseph talked with his brothers,
    but he didn't tell them who he was—not yet.
"Is your father well?" asked Joseph.
"Do you have another brother?"
"Our father is well," they said.
    "We have a younger brother at home."
"When you come again to buy corn," said Joseph,
    "bring your younger brother with you."
Joseph filled their empty sacks with corn,
    and the ten little donkeys went home.

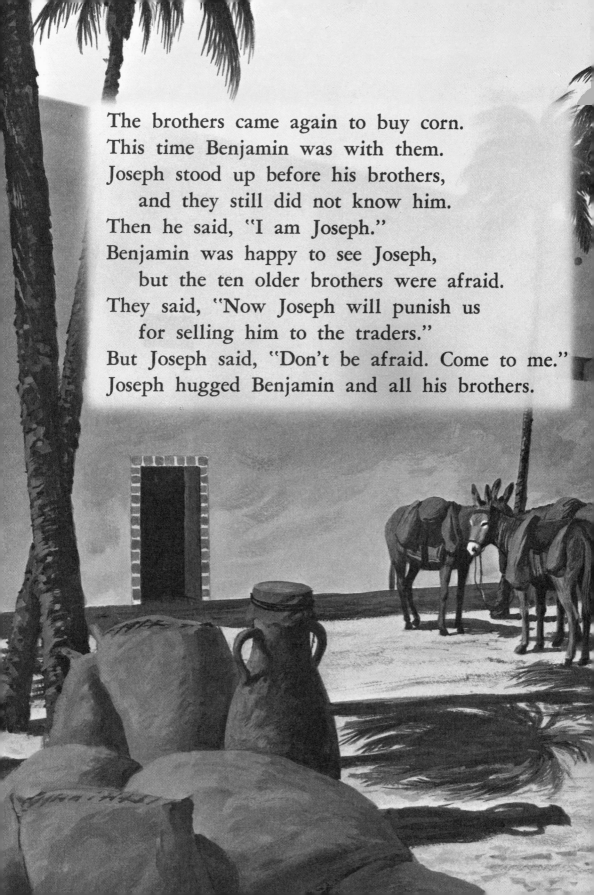

The brothers came again to buy corn.
This time Benjamin was with them.
Joseph stood up before his brothers,
    and they still did not know him.
Then he said, "I am Joseph."
Benjamin was happy to see Joseph,
    but the ten older brothers were afraid.
They said, "Now Joseph will punish us
    for selling him to the traders."
But Joseph said, "Don't be afraid. Come to me."
Joseph hugged Benjamin and all his brothers.

Joseph's brothers were now good, kind men.
They were sorry for what they had done.
Joseph gave each of them a new coat.
He sent home with his brothers many presents
    for Jacob, his father.
He sent wagons to move them all down to Egypt,
    where there was plenty of corn.

Joseph watched the road—
   and one day he saw the wagons he had sent,
   and the ten little donkeys,
   and his brothers with his father's sheep,
   all coming down the road to Egypt.
Joseph jumped into his chariot.
He galloped his horses up the road to meet them.

When Jacob saw Joseph coming
  he climbed down from the wagon.
Joseph jumped down from his chariot.
He ran to his father
  and threw his arms around him.
He hugged him, and hugged him!
Now, Joseph and his father and Benjamin
  and his ten older brothers
  would all live together happily
  in the land of Egypt.